Border Ways

Poems by George Linney, III

©2013, Tobacco Trail Press, North Carolina
www.tobaccotrailchurch.com

ISBN: 978-0-9893321-0-1

Printed in the United States of America by Lightning Source, Inc. P. O. Box 503531, St. Louis, MO 63150-3531 615-213-4491

For Sallie

A special thanks to my mother, Barbara Linney, who has heard and edited each poem, painted the cover art, and cheered and encouraged so that this project could come to fruition. Many, beginning with this son, have written and lived better because of her. Read her life's work at www.turnyourface.com

Contents

Introduction

[I] Beginnings

[II] Away

[III] Home

[IV] Nature

[V] Running

[VI] Endings

Introduction

March 7, 2013

I did not like poetry or have any use for the form when I was young. But all that changed over the last couple of years when the voice kept saying: write poetry.

I have heeled to the repeated commands of the voice before and been glad. Going back almost a decade, Rick Lischer taught me in class once upon a time, *the preacher is the poet for the church.* I accidently perceived his words literally and then when the voice seemed to echo the same charge, before I knew it I was collecting verses in binders, jotting down stanzas on napkins, and filling my time with near rhyme and trying to sing out a line through written words.

As I have studied with the poet and philosopher, David Whyte, once at Duke, and three times in Charleston, I have watched, read, listened and thought, I want to do that, meaning write poetry and reflect on the words and the process.

So I have. And here are the first 36 collected poems.

Sometimes the poetry has been the natural outpouring of serving as pastor among the Tobacco Trail Church. Other times, I have penned as a father or a runner. All the time, I have written as a follower trying to find a way forward along the border of what has come before, what is going on in this current flow, and with a secret hope that these words might prepare me for what is around the corner. I hope you enjoy this work and that just one image might resonate and help you along the river of your own life.

Written inside the binder that has collected these poems along the way is a quote from Rilke that speaks specifically to writing, but can be instructions for anything we want to do:

> "Go into yourself. Search for the reason that bids you write; find out whether it is spreading its roots in the deepest places of your heart, acknowledge to yourself whether you would have to die if it were denied you write. This above all—ask yourself in the stillest hour of your night: *must* I write? Delve into yourself for a deep answer. And if this should be affirmative, if you may meet this earnest question with a strong and simple 'I *must*,' then build your life according to this necessity; your life even into its most indifferent and slightest hour must be a sign of this urge and a testimony to it."

Letters to a Young Poet by Rainer Maria Rilke, p. 18-19.

Rainer Maria Rilke, Letters to a Young Poet, translation by M.D. Herter Norton, New York: 1993, Norton & Company, Inc.

[I]
Beginnings

Photo by Kevin Garrison

Border Ways

Smart as a whip
and just as stubborn
A dozen ages gone by
since birth
behind a mountain dumpster
we found each other in Frisco
ten months later
and together ever since
we have run and fetched
slept and stayed
heeled a few thousand times
strayed a few more
you wander
but to home
you always return

Remember when it was the green truck
our home away from home
you'd find her
and trust
that I would return

Blessing Before Writing

Breathe deeply
calmly
wait...
and then write

Clear your mind
and then look up

Search for The Word
the one word
and then another
do not rush
search for the companion
the link
out there on the horizon
or buried in the sand

Allow them time to be spoken back to you
take the one image and paint it
outside the lines
forget the borders
for now

Do not edit
or judge
or contemplate too deeply

Just chase the image
around the corner
by the tail

Look back
from above
over your shoulder
and then twist and turn down
back onto the page
quiet yourself once more

And write
a while longer

Coffee and Oranges

I wonder if they have healing properties
when combined
like an elixir
mixed and united
for the soul and body.

Can you be in a bad mood
tasting a slice
from a Naval
with a bitter blend?

Fingers smell like cleaner
with no chemicals.

Recharging
Brightening the winter
somehow raising the mercury
but all in the heart
in the imagination
but bright in the belly.

Still in January

We are still in January
but I speak not of time
or its passing
or waiting for Spring
but a state of being
a snippet
caught and revealed

a deep breath
heard in here
by the border
and out there
by the bird

the window is cast open
letting in the true light
and the true sound

and we all listen
me, the dog, the bird
to just our breathing
the exhale of the
others'
the companions'
in this momentary fast
from noise

we have cleared our minds
and the same holds true
for our hearts
our souls

The Window

Moss blows gently in the low country
Charleston
In February
Wants to be warm
But stuck in winter
The Spanish Moss
Moves outside the window
Of the Library
Where an inspirer inspires
Into the great frontier
We shall overcome
Just a crack or a wide-gaping hole
Who's to say
Just open that window
Just a bit ajar
Let the latch fling to an open orientation
And let the wind do what she will
Permit the wind to be the
Flowing dancing skipping skopping
Let Heaney into my soul
Let the poet-priest be who I become
How I am incarnated
Embodied
Shaped and formed

Sophia

Sitting at the edge of a piano
Mold and mildew
Breathing them in
Her old legs
Archaic pedals
A welcome mat to Charleston
The sunshine meanders in through arch-shaped blinds
Is that gothic in form and fashion, structure?

Folks are on edge ready, a good edge
Ready for a good word
Will we get it?
I'm sure we will

Blake, Wordsworth, James, and Rilke
They all bound around in my head
Ready to share a good word
And the lights go down
The sun meanders no more as the blinds are closed

Dickinson, Heaney, Eliot, Kavanagh

What other gifts will be given?
Who will we be gifted with?

I am in great need of a healing
A soul cleansing

Let it come
Rinse over me

Voices

Wind blows
Sun shines
And a woman yells harshly
Emphatically
To someone on the other end of digitized audio waves
The scene is out of concert
Because the day preaches coolness, calmness, serenity
Who needs such a harsh talking to?
I'm glad it's not me
Though I could probably use one
Run faster
Parent better
Work harder
Write with greater clarity

She is calming and walking nearer
Smiling to the person on the other end, though he can't see the smile
Perhaps he can hear it somehow, in the turn of a word
Serenity overcomes me as it has already done on this bright day
by hearing that best part of
Beethoven's Piano Concerto No. 5 in E-flat major, Op. 73
Listen to it and choose your best part
I discovered it again for the first time
In a theater watching a stammerer find his voice
And though afraid of falling on his words into empty space
He went anyway and spoke into the mic
Found his voice and the heart of a nation
You too have a voice
Somewhere there is an audience
That needs your story

[II]
Away

Fourteener along the Boyne

Outside Slane
from Rossnaree
we clopped and clipped
in and out of weather
sideways rain
then sun rays

All the while Boyne flowed
in the valley

Lush is the order of the hour
Wind blows hard in
this tenth month
announcing a shift

Yet here in Ireland green persists
Cattle graze
lean into gusts
on flowing emerald slopes
just as they have
for generations

Panes shake at Rossnaree
as I scribe and soak in
the county Meath

Wind whips over the grass
Picking up speed
as the ground drops
out from underneath the gust
The force of air
loses its surface
the vector keeps it straight
in mid-air
NOW
and it seeks another structure
to engage

Tops of foliage down the hillside
receive a glancing blow
but the big back stop
is Spruce
He's braced and ready
has received a thousand blows
and will not fall

Now here comes the rain
And the temperature drops
or so it looks
from inside mortar and windows
it's cold in here
but not like out there

Come down rain
and wet this Earth
whet my pen

At home the wind
eases back in the rain
but hardly here
the two know each
other all too well
and collaborate and
equate to October
harshness

13

Lament to Sunshine

In my ear
is a *Warning Sign*
from Coldplay

Come on in
I've gotta tell you what a state I'm in…

…when the truth is
I miss you

a hillside for hunting
off to the left

Today, I run the road from Drogheda
wet from a hard rain, but not anymore
now sun is over the horizon at my left
and I sink to 6:30s
why not, for I'm tired but Coldplay works
plays
sings
through the fatigue
I'd do well to do just the same.
I envision them playing at Slane Castle.
It is nearby, but I am not going that way.
Touristy things are not on my list
I have been to Open Farm and down to Duleek Quarry
stopped at the bridge
over the railroad tracks
watched the tractors
churn the earth
while birds seek the afterbirth
of the newly delivered
soil
turned over
I've seen the way these people live—mostly farmers.
It is what I came for.

County Meath

County Meath is filled with gems
    The Castle at Slane, the fight for
        Old Bridge, there are fishermen
           @ Drogheda
                of course there's Brú na Bóinne
                    where graves are marked and short days counted
                    Still
                Boyne flows on and on
            not a care
        for all the fuss
      out to sea she ripples
never naming yet carving the countryside

Check out: www.rossnaree.ie. I wrote this and the two previous poems from the second story of that building looking out over the River Boyne and her lush green pastures.

What Happened in West Virginia

What happened in WV
was a ride on two wheels
up a hill
into the lush green
as the horizon
line
edged upward
False flats
and then up again
Curve and weave
Cut the corners
Or stay to the right
for safety and to abide
by the laws of the land
good laws
better not to surprise oncoming traffic
in a dart
for their lives
and his

The Way

I've not travelled the Way
the Camino
the path in Spain
but I want to.

I want to get lean in a harsh wind
and say few words
while the world speaks to me.

I want to see Saint James
near the coast
and burn my shoes
like I think Moses might have burned his along the way to God.

Santiago de Compostela
it just sounds good
like a place you want to walk
pray
grow hungry
learn from the land

If I had my druthers
I would go along the Way in Lent
and walk for forty days

it would be cold
but that seems fitting, yet frightening
and the crowds would be less
and I would turn inward

and there would be space to enter:
Nel mezzo del cammin di nostra vita
mi ritrovai per una selva oscura,
*ché la diritta via era smarrita.**

In the middle of the road of my life
I awoke in the dark wood
where the true way was wholly lost.

*Dante's first lines in *The Commedia*. Translation unknown.

17

[III]
Home

10/10/03

In 48 my boy will be 8
how can that be
2003 and he was born
while I was on holiday
from Stanley's Christian Ethics

We studied war no more
contraception
marriage and fidelity
worship habits
practices of prayer

But mid-way through holiday,
by this evening, the 8th, a Wednesday,
Kristen was breathing heavy and sleepless
I rested and turns out I'd need it
We'd take it where we could get it

48 hours later he came to the world healthy
affirming much of what I was purposed for
fatherhood
and a few other chores
and calls

He was long like Usain @ 9 lbs 2 ounces
A special boy with a keen eye for the world
soaking it all in always taking in all the stimuli

At seven almost eight, the world is his oyster
He can do it all
Musician, runner, mathematician,
and why not
why not seek them all
Capture this season and ride it out until the next one
comes to you in a flurry

Queen of the Slide

I am queen of the slide
     and no one can stop me
        not the sun
           nor the wind
              not my little brother
                not a friend

I'm queen of the slide
but what do I do
when all my subjects have fled?
Who am I queen of then?
The slide still knows who's boss
but who else?

Perhaps
I will reign over the swings

toddler

A toddler
spins and spins and spins
until dizzy
Smile on face
equilibrium elsewhere...
he spins again

Out of control feels good
trust from somewhere
who knows where
that balance
shall come again

If wobbly
mommy will swoop me up
and clutch me tight
I close my little eyes
and the cosmos comes back into focus

Only that I might spin again

God's kingdom is like this
we trust
that protection is a wide pair of arms
we risk
to prove and test, or just because,
we shall be held

a room that rumbles

To be a grownup
in our clan
kind of an old person
if you ask me
you first need a room that rumbles
I did not have one in college
I did not have one in Summit County
I did not have one in Transylvania County
But now in Durham County
I have a room that rumbles

Rooms rumble
with a cabinet
filled sparingly
at least on some shelves
with China
and never touched candlesticks
and a decanter that never held
and never will hold
Brandy

My mother's house has a room that rumbles
when you walk by, it
sounds
kind of like a wobble bridge
the kind that bows down at an arc
and makes you feel like your knees don't work

In the rumble room
children know that rumble sound without being told
and know not to
play
in that room
so they move along
instinctively

You really do not see bulls in China shops
Even they know better

Both my grandmothers
had their rooms that rumbled

Am I old like them

Their cabinets held ancient artifacts
or so I thought
of Linneys and Johnsons
of days gone by

A room that rumbles
is for sitting still
and sipping tea

How fun is that

not much if you're a kid or still want to be one

If I asked my wife if we could make a change
so this room no longer rumbled
I imagine
she would laugh it off quickly without even a response
as if that were about as likely
to happen
as our next vacation being to Mars

I'm not sure I want a room that rumbles

This House

This house grounds me in ways beyond my understanding.

I'm truly home when I ascend the welcome path
and off to the left with the sun brightening her yellowness are two
stories of the place I call home.
I'm halted by the bricks that lie before me and the Leland's that
shroud the sideline.
I turn to port and roll into the cave.
Sometimes there is a greeter at the door asking to drive with a
word from the day.
But often just an open door to confirm who is rolling in and then a
retreat to play.

She is quiet at times, and noisy in other moments, but she is al-
ways home.
Pictures hang all-around of the places we've been, the people who
rest here, those who share our names and our blood.
We get together and worship God here when days are cold, and
the fire switch is flipped and little ones like Joseph and Eloise
gather on her carpet.
So much food has been shared within her walls and wines poured
and new bottles opened.

The cornerstone must have been laid very carefully. While the
house is not brick, I like to think of it as brick, because then Stan-
ley and his daddy could have laid it. That makes for a good house.

Much ink has been spilled under her roof to tell her story, and
God's story, and my story. But so often, she speaks to me and tells
me the words to write and the images to explore. How does a
house do this? How can she be so hospitable to me? I do not know.
I just know it is true.

Thank you.

In the Piedmont

I.
Rocks are jagged in the Piedmont
but climbable
slip and sutures
may be needed
but skut and scurry over
nimble and sly
you'll be fine

II.
Dogs run loose in the Piedmont
all signs
direct
leashes required
but many disregard
for he must roam
to and fro

III.
Trails are twisty in the Piedmont
Straight lines are out
non-vogue
when land is soft
and rolling
narrow trails
rarely graded
too mundane

IV.
March is Spring in the Piedmont
Sure
cold can return
but crisp and sunny
even hot
more oft
than not

27

V.
Marry Durham in the Piedmont
If perchance
you
heart
her
Why not marry her?
My only polygamy

My Mother's Uncle's Love

Lawrence
brother on daddy's side
tall, six big feet and then some
larger than life to a little girl
Ivory hair with some oomph
not like daddy's or mine,
straighter than we might have liked
His looked like daddy's, but puffed up a bit,
in a good way
Daddy, I loved day to day
Uncle Lawrence, I adored

They loved one another as brothers
who had seen joys and sorrows
Sorrows of another brother, brother, and sister
who lived too few days
Joys of a life of shared food and work and play

At dinner, a Johnson institution
He'd smile across the table
A grin that seemed just for me
He'd flash it again when telling a joke
Or when he'd shock his taste buds
back and forth
with salty country ham
then a sweet morsel
and back to swine
With that smile the whole time
he said one taste called for the other
I never doubted the truth in that
for it seemed
he might walk on water
as easy as he described the nuances of taste buds

From Sabbath Supper we'd retreat
and we were living room bound
I'd sit next to Uncle Laurence
Still the laughing, still the smiling
and the dinner table joke turned to a story
He might tell of a time on horseback
shadowing a parade
keeping the peace
looking at the urban crowd from on high
in our nation's capitol
It was 60 miles north of where I listened,
but it seemed to be another planet
to hear him tell of it
from his vantage
saddled on a steed

The story would wrap around me
and put weights on my eyelids
I'd put my head on his knee
He'd scratch my back
his manicure or lack thereof
made my back tickle at the start
drawing me back from near slumber
but not for long
He'd dance from near shoulder to far
then at my spine
knowing just when to move on
to new pastures
When the back 40 was fully grazed
he moved into a gentle rub
and I'd slip into sleep

He stayed once when mama and daddy went travelin'
I remember the fries
The homemade fries
Long slices of potatoes
slathered in oil
an inferno hazard, I know

The paper towel caught fire
As calm as I imagined him on horseback
He swatted the towel with the slatted spoon
and snuffed it out
He kept the peace by staying at peace, calm to the end

Though I saw him
maybe only twice in a calendar's cycle
Always, I knew
Love
Adoration
He cherished me, that Uncle Lawrence

When he died I'd long since become a woman
But I was taken back to the girl
whose back he took time to scratch
who would always be safe from flames
who had a knight on a white horse
a knight with matching white hair
like her daddy's, but a little different

In the funeral escort
a long line of flashing lit patrol cars
we passed the monuments and all his favorite sites
The District would always be his playground
more than it was the President's home or home to that ivory obelisk
The monuments are fine
but they can't stand up to his gray cardigan sweater
that still probably sniffs of
his aftershave
his cigar
his sweet sweat

[IV]
Nature

Saplings — 1/13/13

these pine tree saplings
know no hindrance
no boundaries
the slant of the berm
serves as no obstacle to their prosperity

a neat and manicured row of Leland Cyprus perch
along the top of the berm
planted seven years ago
and ending with the outcropping of our back deck

yet the pines pop up at will
wherever the pine cones burrow
and the soil and season are just so
others wash or roll away
decaying
into compost
nutrition
for their cousins

old trees fall and the berm is not bothered
aged makes way for the fledgling
across berm's back the old arbores break
from wind and soaked soil
and become giant obstacles
like those in a cross country race
these logs lie dying on the slope
thick grass surrounds the cylinders
buffered in a pale yellow grass in this first month
as the giants grind into the earth

vines choke the elders many feet skyward
fungi spreads in southern humidity
and strips the bark
birds still find sanctuary
high above our home

but the younger trees are not prostrate
or heading that way
one sapling seeks the deep well
where the fastest water flows
under the yard
to the old pond.
the young pines thrive at what was once a watering hole
that now makes space for suburbia

the backyard has become a fishbowl
and we the Betta within

    PLAYGROUND
    SWING
    TRAMPOLINE
    ZIP-LINE

when we arrived in aught six
only dirt to harvest
seeds of grass scalding in the summer sun
but with time and care
green ruled the day.

it's not perfect soil
but what is outside of eden
where is such rich soil that does not rest under trees at Moreh or Mamre

the yard needs mulch or maybe not
by winter's mark the yard thrives
thanks to Kristen's toil

and will glow in the fiery colors of Spring
if we will wait

A Home Awaits

A Home Awaits
I checked her today
but empty still
hanging near chutes and ladders
from beams with swings
over wood chips and decaying grass

Weathered and unstained
except for the stains
of her last guests

If only she were filled
would know Spring is here
or just round the corner
but it is the second month
too soon
despite dips skyward in the mercury

Cousins make noise and sing to one another
but it is too soon
to seek a den for mating and passing down generations

My heart longs for grey to turn to green
Yellow stalks and shoots cannot be gleaned or gathered
it is too soon

When will you come Spring
And bloom
Yearning for your color
Your greens and reds

Empty home
Soon you will be filled with eggs and mouths
feather and straw
molting and rotting

skin and feathers
how beautiful
Squawking chirping begging for sustenance
will be the faint sounds muffled inside your home
Come home and announce your Earth's revolution
and tipping
round the axis of the Sun

Tuesday Verses

I awoke early with Cassidy on my mind
it was reading time
would I make it to the quarters workout?
who is to say
instead
I waited for another day or later in this one
rather
I looked out on the tall green pines and the bright sunshine
oh March
you mean Spring in the Piedmont
birds are dancing
I know the blue ones are working on their new house
there goes a cardinal
Kathryn says the males are brown
I didn't know that.

The Wild Roses

Blooming
they can't be contained
never thought they would
unleashed
revolting from dormancy
no one can stop them
no one can contain them
they bleed on a green backdrop
no matter that I see them behind black iron bars
that's just a fence
with a gate for me
but for these buds
they will grow through if they so desire
perhaps even clinging and wrapping
becoming one

Vines @ Foster's Market

A *September Morn* with The Diamond in my ear,
    as he so often enters my virtual cochlea in times of peace and calm
Little gray birds chirp and play,
    frolicking in the late summer sun,
    wish I knew them by name and species,
    but ornithology and nomenclature never were my gifts
A BP across the way is the only eye sore,
    but too much beauty drowns out the hideous green canopy

Gaze returns to aesthetic details more pleasing to the eye and ear

This forest green rocking swing,
    the kind that glides only straight back and straight forward,
    like the sofa on the William Street back porch
    home of William and Ruby Lee
Above this gentle rocker, the one where I rock today
    a canopy of vines,
    weaving over conversations and thoughts
    gently covering with arms stretched out in protection from the elements
    for those who take the time to sit in calm beneath the vines and branches
    making shade enough to stay outside @ Foster's
    and relish in the buzz of cicadas
    still a signal of summer in the South
The vines remind of John's Gospel,
    Where Is It? I must find The Way there
    Ah, there it is,
    the 15th chapter and the 5th verse,
    "I the vine, you the branches"
Thanks Big 'J' for Vines @ Foster's Market

Down by da tree

We gathered
in the shade
her spines like the long bows
sweeping and curving
make the circle dense dripline
40 x 40
for the four of us and more
for our sitting

It is the willow tree
Give thanks for the willow tree

She says, come
and sit
stay and listen
hear the wind
feel the sun
listen to the welcome from the drum

Heart beatin'
Foot thumpin'
Land shakin'

Birds are Busy

Birds are busy in the morning

A fat cardinal flies low from fence to branch

Out of the reeds and rushes flits a brown one

Thrushes skirt the playground and perch on a tall pine

Blue bird seeks his mate guarding the eggs

White moon falling sees all

While fall threatens on a mild August morn

Green is abundant on this piedmont landscape

Good camo for these wing-ed friends

Turning on Time

She used to turn in July
seemingly not knowing
the time
and the season

Now she turns on time
just now the grassy hues turn to
chestnut
crimson
canary

Is it the four years of maturity
watching out over the land on this welcome path
this Forest Brook, she sits on high ground

When she first took root
why did she fall early

It is October in the Piedmont
and the time is on time for dipping temps
and falling leaves

[V]
Running

12/29/11

I wish I had run at Uwharrie
between Christmas and the 31st
but I will
in the 2nd month
on the 4th day
and it will be swift
less than an hour

I have tried twice before
in 64 and 61

It is easier said than done
the minutes pass so quickly

Over the first hill
not as much trouble
as all the fuss
critical not to be overdressed
when you summit
and the sun is at your left
that's when you know who is fit
either
you are
or you are not

Then start dodging trees
and planting feet on tops of
leaves
hopping and hoping
searching
for good and powerful ground
much unseen
just trusted

It's breakneck for a while

I'm sure it is the uphills
for me
which must be faster
if I hope to achieve

Perhaps I will run Uwharrie
again
early in the first month
it is worth the trouble
to prepare and get set
to go

Little River Plan

Easy down to the cabin, tuck in rhythmically.
Fast mile, under 6min
Up the hills hard then hustle and flow down the trail to the river
Create some separation
Make some folks worry about what is up this cold morning

Short strides up the steep hill
back to the aid station
relax
recover
cruise down to the wooden board walk and out to the fire road
flow back onto the single track
hustle calmly down to the river and over the bridges

Running Up the Slope

On the way to Imperial Bowl
One of many summits in this Summit County
This "green" seemed steep facing it in reverse
I trudged in my snowshoes
Knowing Jon was at the top
Waiting to be tagged
Ready to race down and down and down
I tried to manage my breathing
Not redline
But it was tough
Every step took me to higher elevation
Less oxygen
More calf squeezing from the vectors pointing up and up
I love the name of this slope—CLAIM JUMPER
It tells a story of old gold miners with their pans
And squinty eyes
Looking for treasure
For me, it reminds of my first breakfast in Colorado
At the Frisco restaurant carrying the same name
Good coffee and eggs and hash browns
Weighting down my guts for a day of riding down and down and down

[VI]
Endings

Now and Then

At the border
Just shy of the edge
Of here and there

we have come to a cross
and one of us must sit
and one of us must stand
contemplating the necessary posture
accepting that we must take the position we can and no other
not now
for now we can play but one part
in the drama

At the precipice
Between living now
And dying then
from one to the next is but a passing
through to a wonderful new world

The flap of light shimmers as it closes over her
Shelling her in like a pearl
Inside the oyster

she can see partially dimly barely
through to the source of the illumination
outside the protected hide

a kind of borderland
cloaked inside this tomb
but able to see out
to yearn for the other side
while dangerously safe and protected within

outside is everything
but here, close in
right next to her heart
is most of the work
the abundance
fecundity fertility fruit bearing possibility

but she must venture out to partner
and risk everything
everything held dear
crossing the border
stepping across the cliff
the ceiling must erupt

momentarily
and then the opportunity
to revert to home

Hearing

there is a rattle in my ear
and in my throat
a low thump that pulses and persists as pressure that will not deflate

we have ruled out a clot, a bleed, a tumor
i guess it is just a virus
lodged where i cannot see between lobes and brain
nothing glamorous
though persisting now a fortnight

two weeks into this flow
six total weeks of sickness
four antibiotics
steroids
and ear drops

God make it end
i cannot hear my voice

is it too much to ask to be among the hearers when i play the speaker?
i suppose so

pitch, tone, volume is off or at least it is to my ear
others say raspy, but not in a good way

you must want it this way
i never understand your ways

return me to november or perhaps early april
for that i would be grateful

i feel like i'm in a fishbowl
straining to speak and bubbles must be floating to the surface as i muscle
to force this muffled projectile—a sorry excuse for a voice as it were
hardly arcing anywhere
but puttering out barely passing over my lips

i cannot hear my voice
and it has been two weeks

the best days are the days with few words so i'm not reminded of
my inadequacy

it is exhausting
the inquiries
how are you?
though i am grateful for the caring while resenting the hell out of it
and i go on
and time has told me
this too shall pass

today was among the best of days
i read and i wrote under your provision
mostly in silence
and yet how much i did hear
the other kind of hearing
that which comes without sound

you always make space for something else
the other
if only we would turn to smell, taste, touch, and sight

Immunity Down

All over the world
Patients wander halls with IV stands
Wheeling around with that one wheel
like at the grocery store
that will not roll.
The patients are mobile
and appear free
but with an asterisk.
No longer will oral meds suffice.
They need an umbilical cord
of a cocktail no one would ever order.

Heeler, Not Healer

It's not that there is anything wrong with a healer
we all need one
and He is one
The One,
for that matter

but for now
I am dreaming of Jesus as heeler
the one who stays by my side
Is it too much, too much to imagine that God would condescend to
the role of a dog who comes to my side at the rising of the sun?
asking,
what can I do for you today?

I don't know...perhaps I speak out of turn.
But maybe we could suspend pleasantries and formalities
so that we all might be one, praying better
if we imagined Jesus saying these very words
What can I do for you today?
What does our work look like?
How can I pray for you this morning?

When I would leave the property at the farm I inhabited
the dog would hear the truck and heel at the side of the tire, at 10 or
even 25 miles per hour, looking left to confirm that I was the driver.
She would risk a torn achilles to stay abreast of the green ford ranger.
At the road I would have to thank her, order her, to stay.

I will be back
and she would retreat
to I don't know what
other sheep?
a place of waiting?
so often I would drive up and she would be there, even if I pulled into
another entrance.
How is this not like Jesus' presence, his heeling, in my life?
There when I need him, begging to come along side me and show me
the way.
Sure, in the bigger sense, in the truer sense, He is my master, my Lord,
but why, how did it come to be?
Because he laid down his life for my own.
Like the dog would do for me.

Dog Gone

The dog days are over
It is done
And it is sad
All that hair
On clothes and cars
Lighter than feathers
How long will I find these sheds
Painful reminders of how good you were
Loyal and true
Humble and obedient
We took you for granted
But never the reverse
Life's not fair for a puppy
But it is simple
You don't ask for much
More begs for love than for food
How we squandered you
And yet, you never us
You will be missed
Is there a heaven for dogs, in my mind, there must be
You have all the attributes to get there

Wall

I want to build a wall
along the berm
It might take months
even years
one rock at a time
sometimes three or four
with the help of the little ones.
They might want to use it
so they might as well
help build it.

I want to build a wailing wall
or a shouting wall
or a singing wall
maybe a dancing wall
all based on the month.
It will curve up and over and
along the spine of the berm
from down by the trampoline
all the way to the first Leland Cyprus
or is that the last?

It will take different stacks and all kinds of rocks
because the berm's at differing heights
but when it is done
it will be level and flat
and solid for sitting
or for crying
or for kneeling

Just like our ancestors
we will place our supplications
and let the wall do its work.

For more information about seminars, retreats or speaking engagements, please contact:

George Linney, III
3212 Denada Path
Durham, NC 27702
(919) 414-6565
www.tobaccotrailchurch.com
revgeorgelinney@gmail.com

CPSIA information can be obtained at www.ICGtesting.com
Printed in the USA
BVOW102033040613

322391BV00004B/4/P